CHRISTY MATHEWSON

BARRY BONDS

BUCK EWING

WILLIE MAYS

MEL OTT

BILL TERRY

JUAN MARICHAL

ROSS YOUNGS

WILLIE McCOVEY

JEFF KENT

GAYLORD PERRY

ORLANDO CEPEDA

THE HISTORY OF THE
SAN FRANCISCO
GIANTS

AARON FRISCH

CREATIVE C EDUCATION

Published by Creative Education, 123 South Broad Street, Mankato, MN 56001

Creative Education is an imprint of The Creative Company.

Designed by Rita Marshall.

Photographs by AllSport (Otto Greule, Harry How, Jed Jacobsohn), Associated Press/Wide World

Photos, Icon Sports Media (John Cordes), National Baseball Library, SportsChrome

(Jeff Carlick, Rob Tringali Jr.)

Library of Congress Cataloging-in-Publication Data

Frisch, Aaron. The history of the San Francisco Giants / by Aaron Frisch.

p. cm. — (Baseball)   ISBN 978-1-58341-223-7

Summary: A team history of the Giants, who arrived in San Francisco in 1958 from

New York, where they had played for seventy-five years.

1. San Francisco Giants (Baseball team)—History—

Juvenile literature. [1. San Francisco Giants (Baseball team)—History.

2. Baseball—History.] I. Title. II. Baseball (Mankato, Minn.).

GV875.S34 F75 2002   796.357'64'0979461—dc21   2001047874

9 8 7 6 5 4 3

SAN FRANCISCO,

CALIFORNIA, WAS FOUNDED IN 1776 AS A SMALL

Spanish mission. Although the city gained fame as a destination

for fortune seekers during the great gold rush of 1848, today it is

best known for its striking beauty and booming tourism industry.

San Francisco sits atop a series of steep hills surrounded on three

sides by water, and its soaring bridges and famous cable cars are

often shrouded in a dense fog.

That fog adds a certain air of mystery to San Francisco. For

years, it also added to the unique atmosphere of baseball games at

Candlestick Park, the city's major-league baseball stadium. For four

decades, Candlestick Park was home to the San Francisco Giants, a

team that relocated to the West Coast in 1958. Since then, the team

ROGER CONNOR

5

has lived up to its name, looming large in the National League (NL).

{THE "BIG FELLOWS" BEGIN} The Giants' history began

long before the franchise settled in San Francisco. In

1883, the team played in New York City and was

known by several names, including the Gothams and

the Nationals. The team played its home games just

north of the city's Central Park on an open field

Starring on New York's **1883** squad was infielder John Ward, who stole a whopping 111 bases.

known as the Polo Grounds.

New York was one of baseball's most powerful teams in those

years. The club was led by catcher Buck Ewing, known for his great

speed and all-around skills. New York fans loved watching Ewing,

and he loved showing off for them. During one game, he singled in

the 10th inning and proceeded to steal both second and third base.

He then turned and shouted to the crowd, "It's getting late. I'm

going to steal home, and then we can all have dinner." A few pitches

ROBB NEN

A .303 career hitter, star Buck Ewing was also known for his cannon throwing arm.

BUCK EWING

later, Ewing slid safely across the plate for the win. Such heroics would eventually earn Ewing a place in the Hall of Fame.

The team's manager during that time, James Mutrie, was proud of Ewing and other stars such as first baseman Roger Connor. As the players took the field, he would cheer them on by shouting, "Come on, my big fellows, my giants!" A local sportswriter heard Mutrie and started using the name in the papers. By 1885, the team was officially known as the Giants.

Swift outfielder Mike Tiernan crossed home plate 147 times in **1889**, a club record that still stands.

The Giants finished atop the NL in 1888 and 1889, but they faded in the standings in the 1890s despite the efforts of such players as pitcher Amos Rusie. Finally, in the early 1900s, the Giants turned things around again. Sparking that improvement was John McGraw, a tough infielder who took control of the team in 1902 as a player/manager.

MIKE TIERNAN

Scenic Pacific Bell Park was built along the shore of beautiful San Francisco Bay.

PAC BELL PARK

{McGRAW AND THE MIGHTY GIANTS} The Giants were

the worst team in the NL when McGraw arrived, but just two years

later, they stood atop the league once again. Leading

the team's resurgence were two pitchers: Joe

McGinnity and Christy Mathewson. McGinnity was

called the "Iron Man" because he never seemed to get

tired. Three times in August 1903, he pitched both

games of doubleheaders and won all six contests.

McGinnity was outstanding, but Mathewson was even better.

Combining a rocket fastball and a sweeping curve with a pitch

called a screwball, Mathewson mowed down opposing batters at a

record pace. By the end of his career, he boasted 373 victories and

more than 2,500 strikeouts. "There never was any pitcher like

Mathewson," said McGraw. "And I doubt there ever will be."

New York won the 1905 World Series, and more great players

CHRISTY MATHEWSON

stepped forward to keep the Giants among the NL's elite over

the next two decades. Among them were infielders Frankie Frisch

and George Kelly and outfielder Ross Youngs. The Giants were

practically unstoppable in the early 1920s, beating Babe Ruth's

powerful New York Yankees in both 1921 and 1922 to win back-to-

back World Series championships.

McGraw finally stepped down as manager in 1932. During his

31 years at the helm, the mighty Giants captured 10 NL pennants

In **1933**, Carl Hubbell pitched 46 straight score- less innings en route to a 1.66 ERA for the year.

and three World Series titles. As Philadelphia Athletics

manager Connie Mack once said, "There has been only

one manager, and his name is John McGraw."

{NEW HEROES, MORE TITLES} Although

New York didn't have the leadership of McGraw in

the 1930s, it did have plenty of talent. Three players in particular

stood out during that era: first baseman Bill Terry, pitcher Carl

Hubbell, and outfielder Mel Ott.

Terry, who served as player/manager for five seasons, was a

great fielder and an even better hitter. In 1930, he put together an

amazing .401 batting average. Hubbell, meanwhile, established

himself as the greatest Giants hurler since Mathewson. Like

Mathewson, the left-handed Hubbell tied opposing batters in knots

J.T. SNOW

with a wicked screwball and uncanny accuracy.

Ott joined the Giants in 1926 at the age of 17. The youngster

had one of the league's strangest batting styles. As the ball arrived at

the plate, he lunged toward the mound and snapped his bat at the

ball. Some coaches wanted to change Ott's style, but McGraw

wouldn't let them. "Do what's comfortable for you," the manager advised. Once again, McGraw proved to be right. Before Ott

retired, he rang up an astounding 511 home runs, becoming just the

third player to break the 500-home run mark.

In 1933, these players led New York all the way

to the top. The Giants won the NL pennant, then

beat the American League champion Washington

Senators to win the World Series. New York followed

up its championship by winning league pennants again in 1936 and

1937. But in the 1940s, age began to take its toll on the team's stars,

and the Giants fell into a decade-long slump.

{MIRACLES AND THE "SAY HEY KID"} The Giants broke

out of their slump in dramatic fashion in 1951. That season, the

Giants won 37 of their last 44 games to pull into a first-place tie

with the Brooklyn Dodgers and force a special three-game playoff

series. After the teams split the first two games, Giants outfielder

Mel Ott led New York in home runs for an incredible 18 consecutive seasons (from **1928** to **1945**).

MEL OTT

Third baseman Matt Williams followed in Mel Ott's footsteps as a standout slugger.

Bobby Thomson crushed a dramatic three-run home run in the

bottom of the ninth inning to win game three and give New York

the NL pennant. The round-tripper went down in

history as the "Shot Heard 'Round the World."

A second miraculous play was added to Giants lore

just three seasons later. That year, the Giants again

reached the World Series, where they faced the favored

Cleveland Indians. In the first game of the series, a new Giants hero

was born: young center fielder Willie Mays.

The score was tied 2–2 in the eighth inning, and Cleveland

had two runners on base when Indians slugger Vic Wertz sent a

blast to the deepest part of center field. It seemed certain the shot

would sail over Mays, but he raced straight away from home plate

and made an impossible over-the-shoulder catch. He then whirled

around and fired the ball back to the infield to hold the runners in

Outfielder Willie Mays slammed 660 career homers, the third-most in major-league history.

WILLIE MAYS

place. The stunned Indians never seemed to recover from that play,

and the Giants went on to win the World Series.

Mays became as popular off the field as he was on it. The

friendly slugger loved to talk, but he had a terrible time remembering

names. He playfully hid his problem by using the all-purpose greeting

"Say hey." Before long, Mays became known as the "Say Hey Kid," a star many consider the greatest all-around player in baseball history. "He could do the five things you have to do to be a superstar:

Orlando Cepeda won fans over in **1961** by going deep 46 times and driving in 142 runs.

hit, hit with power, run, throw, and field," said Giants manager Leo Durocher. "And . . . he lit up the room when he came in. He was a joy to be around."

{WEST-COAST WINNERS} Sadly, New York fans got to watch Mays for only a few seasons. In 1958, poor fan attendance prompted the Giants to pack up and move to San Francisco. There, several new stars emerged, including young first baseman Orlando Cepeda, slugging outfielder Willie "Stretch" McCovey, and pitcher Juan Marichal. In 1962, these players led San Francisco to the NL pennant with a 103–62 record. Unfortunately, the Giants could not bring home a World Series trophy, losing to the New York Yankees in seven games.

Pitcher Gaylord Perry helped the Giants remain among the NL's

ORLANDO CEPEDA

All-Star Gaylord Perry led all NL hurlers in innings pitched in **1969** and **1970**.

GAYLORD PERRY

best in the late 1960s, but the team couldn't quite reach the top.

Then, in the early '70s, Mays and McCovey were traded away.

The Giants brought in an array of talented young players—including outfielder Bobby Bonds, shortstop Chris Speier, and starting pitcher John "the Count" Montefusco—in an attempt to rebuild, but the team slid down the standings.

In **1969**, outfielder Willie McCovey became the fifth Giants player to win the NL MVP award.

The Giants continued to struggle until 1986. That year, San Francisco was led by new manager Roger Craig and featured a much-improved lineup that included outfielder Candy Maldonado, first baseman Will Clark, and second baseman Robby Thompson. Craig told reporters that his team was going back to the basics. "If we can discipline ourselves to do the little things right," he said, "the big things will take care of themselves."

In 1987, the Giants' devotion to the basics paid off as the team

WILLIE McCOVEY

won its first NL Western Division title in 16 years (the league was split into two divisions in 1969). The Giants then took on the St. Louis Cardinals in the NL Championship Series for the right to

advance to the World Series. Unfortunately, the Giants came up just short, losing the series in seven games.

Two years later, Clark and slugging outfielder Kevin Mitchell led the Giants all the way to the World Series, where they faced

their neighbor from across the bay, the powerful Oakland Athletics.

Baseball experts predicted an exciting series, but no

one could have predicted the drama that would

unfold. As the teams prepared to play game three in

Candlestick Park, an earthquake rocked the Bay Area.

The destruction it caused forced the series to be

Will Clark was awarded the Gold Glove award in **1991** in recognition of his stellar defense.

postponed for 10 days, and the Giants were ultimately swept by the

A's in one of the most bizarre World Series ever.

{BONDS BOMBS AWAY} After two mediocre seasons,

the Giants brought in new manager Dusty Baker in 1992. In an

attempt to bring the sleeping Giants to life, the team also signed

former Pittsburgh Pirates outfielder Barry Bonds. The move was

a brilliant—and fitting—one. Not only was Bonds a two-time NL

Most Valuable Player (MVP), but he was also the son of former

WILL CLARK

Giants star Bobby Bonds and the godson of the great Willie Mays.

Bonds could do it all. He had a rifle of an arm from left field,

Pitcher John Burkett went 22–7 in **1993** as the Giants reached their highest win total in 31 seasons.

and his great speed made him a top-notch base stealer. But his best feature was his mighty left-handed stroke at the plate. Unlike most sluggers, Bonds choked up several inches on the bat. But his powerful arms enabled him to whip the bat around with incredible

speed. In 1993, he jacked 46 home runs, drove in 123 runs, and stole 29 bases—numbers that earned him a third NL MVP award.

Behind Bonds, third baseman Matt Williams, and intimidating closer Rod Beck, the Giants soared to a 103–59 record in 1993 but narrowly missed the playoffs. The team then fell off track with three straight losing seasons before returning to the top of the NL West in 1997. Bonds and Beck remained the team's leaders, but the Giants also featured such additions as sure-gloved first baseman

JOHN BURKETT

J.T. Snow and powerful second baseman Jeff Kent.

Under Baker's steady guidance, San Francisco remained near

the top of its division throughout the late 1990s.

In 2000, the team left Candlestick Park for the new

Pac Bell Park. Kent had a sensational season in the

new stadium, batting .334 with 33 home runs and

winning the NL MVP award. A year later, powerful

shortstop Rich Aurelia and pitchers Robb Nen and Livan

Hernandez helped keep the Giants flying high.

Rich Aurelia and his teammates were brilliant in the field in **2000**, committing only 93 errors.

The 2001 season truly belonged to Bonds, however. The

veteran slugger was a terror at the plate, slamming 73 home runs

(about one per every six and a half at-bats) to break the major-

league record of 70 set three years earlier by St. Louis Cardinals

slugger Mark McGwire. More amazing was that he did it despite

being walked a major-league record 177 times! "This was one of the

RICH AURELIA

An RBI machine, Jeff Kent knocked in at least 100 runs a season from **1997** to **2001**.

JEFF KENT

One of the all-time greats, Barry Bonds combined a keen eye with uncanny strength.

BARRY BONDS

greatest years—no, it was *the* greatest year—I have seen from a single person," marveled Baker.

Flame-thrower Felix Rodriguez was expected to be a key relief pitcher in the seasons ahead.

No matter where they have played, whether on the East Coast or the West Coast, the Giants have always stood tall. Eighteen NL pennants and five World Series trophies attest to the franchise's success, as do the 28 former greats enshrined in the Baseball Hall of Fame. Settled in Pac Bell Park and supported by the San Francisco faithful, today's Giants plan to soon add to those numbers.

FELIX RODRIGUEZ